DESIGNED
FOR
SUCCESS

A motivational Book
For Today's "Ark-Builder"

EBENEZER AJITENA

EMMANUEL HOUSE
London, United Kingdom

Designed for Success
Copyright © 2000 by Ebenezer Ajitena
Reprinted 2001

Published by
Emmanuel House
PO Box 15022
London
SE57ZL
www.emmanuel-house.co.uk

All scriptures, unless otherwise stated, are taken from
the *King James Version* of the Bible.

ISBN 1 900529 12 2

Cover design by *Himpressions*
Printed in England

Contents

Acknowledgments

I give glory and honour to the Lord for the privilege of a wonderful call into His service. Thank you Father.

My sincere appreciation goes to my brother and friend, Pastor Lanre Obey, whose life has blessed my family and me. He encouraged me to start writing and I thank God for the result of his motivation.

I appreciate the support of my darling wife, Cecilia, and all my children. You are noble vessels in God's hand. I thank you all.

To my mentors, motivators, leaders and encouragers: Pastor J.A. Adelakun, Evangelist (Dr.) Ebenezer Obey and Pastor Matthew Ashimolowo - I thank you sirs.

My gratitude to all my partners in ministry and the entire CLIWOM family. You are exceptional.

Dedicated to my God,
the Almighty Master Designer,
who gave me the
insight and revelation in this book.
He is the Source of my inspiration
and the reason for my ability.
Blessed be the name of the Lord.

Introduction

As a pastor, I have the opportunity to meet and counsel people on a regular basis. Many of the people I interact with face difficulties in different areas of their lives. I have also discovered a yearning for purpose in the hearts of some. Others settle for the status quo.

I have thus concluded, out of my years of walking with the Lord, personal experiences, and ministering to people, that the key to every difficulty in life is *wisdom.*

"Wisdom is the principal thing; therefore get wisdom: and with all thy getting get understanding" (Proverbs 4:7).

God's wisdom is the door to success in life, and this wisdom is stored in the pages of Scripture. When you distance yourself from God's you are inviting failure into your life.

In this book, *Designed for Success,* I have highlighted wisdom from the experiences of

Noah. He succeeded where everyone else failed. As a "modern-day ark-builder", read this book with expectation. You will be *inspired* to build according to God's directives, *empowered* to ride the storms of life, and *equipped* to relate with the various kinds of people who will enter your "ark" of success. *The ark is your life; be determined to build it to the glory of your Maker.*

God wants you to excel because you are *designed for success.*

- Rev. Ebenezer Ajitena

1   *God's Blueprint*

IN every fruit there is a seed and in every seed there is a potential forest. No man is born on earth without a purpose, but when purpose for living is not identified, existence is meaningless.

You can either invest your seeds or consume them. Resist the temptation to "eat" both fruit and seed at the same time. Apply godly wisdom: *eat* and *share* the fruit and *plant* the seed.

Planting is different from killing. You kill a seed when you expose it to corruption and damages before planting. A corrupt seed has limited chances of survival. *If you kill your seed, there is no hope for a harvest.*

There is a divine seed in you. Are you aware of it? Can you answer these questions specifically: *Who am I? Why am I living? What is my purpose in life?* It is amazing how many do not have definite answers for these definite questions.

You need to know who you are. The opinion of your parents about you is not final. What people call you is not important. *See yourself through the eyes of God.*

Jacob knew himself in the light of his past. He sojourned with a history of treachery, dubiousness and cunningness. Now old enough to be a grandfather, he did not have a revelation of purpose.

All these negatives changed the day he set himself apart and wrestled with God. His name and identity changed from Jacob the "swindler" to Israel the Prince.

Do not settle for a mistaken identity. Are you called "Jacob" instead of "Israel"? People may call you "Rahab the harlot" without any knowledge of your future worth. Your potential for success is not dependent on your name ("Jabez", for instance) or history of "sorrow".

God is not a respecter of opinions but of principles. He is not bothered about your colour or race. He is only concerned about His covenant with you. It does not matter whether you are a Moabite named "Ruth", what matters is that you are accepted in Bethlehem!

Did your parents consider you "a mistake"? Are you a victim of circumstances? Were you rejected and abandoned from birth? Did you lack parental care? Are you broken with bitterness, loneliness or the pains of polygamy? What is important *now* is for you to understand your existence from God's perspective.

God created you for a purpose. *You* are fearfully and wonderfully made. You are unique and different from everybody else. God created you for signs and wonders. You are an *original* created without a duplicate. You have God-given ability and potential to influence nations for Christ.

Take a look at yourself in the mirror and glance at your belly. You are heavily "pregnant" with ideas and dreams. You are about to give birth to something great. People are waiting to congratulate and rejoice with you for the birth of purpose.

Every pregnant woman prepares for the arrival of her new baby. It is your time to prepare. You need to get ready. Something great is about to happen in your life! It happened in Noah's life; it will happen in yours.

You Need a Blueprint

God was mindful of Noah's faithfulness. He decided to preserve him and his family through the storms that would wipe away the earth. In order to ride the storms, God commanded Noah to build an ark and gave him the blueprint for constructing it. *If you would ride the storms of life, you need blueprints for your ark.*

Have you asked God for the blueprints of your purpose? If you haven't, create time to make this all-important enquiry. Put everything else on hold until you receive your blueprints from God.

Your parents do not have the "blueprints" of your life. Your friends don't either. No eye has seen it yet; no ear has heard of it; no mind has perceived it. God alone has a copy of your blueprints. *Stay connected, therefore, to your*

Source and receive a revelation of your purpose in God.

You will soon find out that the Master's blueprints for your life is specifically designed for you. It contains detailed specifications you have to follow for success. If you work according to *His* description, you will maximise your potential and fulfil destiny. Rise up now and follow the pattern God reveals to you.

Settle *only* for God's blueprints for your life and stop imitating someone else. *Do not try to be what you are not or you will forget who you are.* Discover your reason for living and be happy at being *you.*

What has the Lord laid in your heart? You do not have to be what people say you are. Find out who you *really* are from your Creator. The manufacturer alone knows the details of His products. You are God's product. You are God's work of art.

<u>WISDOM PRINCIPLES</u>

*In every fruit there is a seed and
in every seed there is a harvest.*

*Do not allow your past to
rob you of your future.*

Stay connected to your Source.

There is no better you than yourself.

You are best doing what you are designed for.

*The blueprints of your life is God's
operational manual for your success.*

*What God purposes for you to do,
He has given to no one else.*

2

You Are Under Construction

W HEN you know God's purpose for your life, what He has called you to do, the Master Designer goes ahead to imprint on your heart a custom-made "success manual". With this manual, you can now build on the foundational knowledge of your purpose. Apostle Paul wrote,

> *"According to the grace of God which is given unto me, as a wise **master-builder**, I have laid the foundation and another buildeth thereon, but **let every man take heed how he buildeth thereon**"* (1 Corinthians 3:10).

Can you visualise "success" in your mind? Are you ready to construct your "success ark"? Have you counted the cost? Will you pay the price of achievement? Realise from the start that your purpose is going to demand from you *commitment* and *hard work.*

God, the Initiator

Now, God initiated the building of Noah's ark. He gave him specific construction details. In the same way, your life's purpose, which originated in the mind of God, is under construction. God has all the details for the building of your life. *As an obedient "Ark Builder", you cannot afford to work things out by your own strength.* Let God be the first and last in all you do, delight in His leading and He will grant you the desire of your heart.

As you follow God's directives in life, you will discover, and will need to develop, the art *of creativity.* God is creative. *"In the beginning God created..."* (Genesis 1:1).

To be a successful "builder" in life, you must understand God's creative concept. Everything ends well that starts and progresses with God. Without God, nothing is beautiful because He makes all things beautiful in its time.

Instructions For Building Your Ark

God will not only initiate the building of your ark. He will guide you through the entire process until completion. From the specific instructions that God gave Noah, we can gain insight to how we should build our lives.

The instruction God gave to Noah was:

"Make thee an ark of Gopher wood; Rooms shalt thou make in the ark..." (Genesis 6:14).

There are some important principles to note in this verse.

It's Your Ark

Firstly, God said to Noah, *"make thee an ark"*.

God does not need an ark to survive a flood. He can walk on water and sleep in the midst of a storm. Like a "flood", He raises high standards against the enemy's rage. The ark was necessary for the survival of Noah, his family and the animal kingdom.

The "ark" God will command you to build is for you, your family and others around you. Without an ark built to God's specifications, you may not survive the storms of life.

Use "Gopher Wood"

Secondly, notice that God specified for Noah the type of wood for the ark, *"Gopher wood"*. Many times we mess up God's instructions by doing things our own way. God's instructions, however, are non-negotiable.

"Partial" obedience is "zero" obedience. Absolute submission to God's will is required for positive results. Do not act like Naaman the Syrian who attempted to write a prescription for the Physician. *Absolute obedience facilitates divine intervention.* If God requires "Gopher wood", then use only Gopher wood!

God gives instructions for different purposes. When He needed an "ark" to preserve baby Moses on the river Nile, He used "an ark of Bulrushes". When He needed an "ark of testimony" that would symbolise His presence among the children of Israel, He specified "an Ark of Shittim Wood". For an ark that will stay afloat the flood and storm, He instructed the construction of an "Ark of Gopher Wood".

Do not use "mahogany wood" to construct your "ark" because it is *readily available*. Neither use the "cedar of Lebanon" because it is *superior in quality*. Use "Gopher wood" because it is *commanded by God!*

Not every good idea is God's idea. Although any other wood can successfully build an ark, only the one specified by God will survive the storms of life. Whatever direction God indicates is the best way to follow.

"Trust in the Lord with all your heart and lean not on your own understanding; in all your ways acknowledge Him, and He will direct your path" (Proverbs 3:5-6).

"Gopher wood" may be rare and dear, but know that God provides for every vision He gives. He will give you everything necessary for the execution of your vision once it is in line with His purpose. He can supply all your needs according to His riches in Christ Jesus.

God will not pay a bill He did not incur. If you buy your "construction materials" from the devil's workshop, God will not pay for them. You are not allowed to build with self-generated raw materials either. God wants you to depend absolutely on Him. *If you can reach your destination without God, then He did not send you in the first place!*

Make Rooms

The third thing to note in God's words to Noah is the instruction, *"Rooms shall thou make in the ark"*. Remember that in principle, the ark is your life and it is meant for you, your family and others around you. *The standard of comfort and orderliness you wish to experience in running the affairs of your life depends on how many "rooms" you are able to make.*

God did not give Noah a specific number of rooms to build in the ark. He only told him to "make rooms". How many "rooms" will you make in your life? I will like to suggest some:

God

It is said, "Give God the biggest room in you life". Better still, as the Bishop of your soul, let God have access to every room in your life. Give everything you have and own to Him. He is knocking on the door of your heart. Open up and welcome His presence. Your body is His temple. Let your life be God's permanent dwelling-place.

Integrity

Understand that to be great in life, integrity is compulsory. Make "room" for integrity in your "ark". If you want to go for the best God has intended for you, be a person of integrity.

"The integrity of the upright shall guide them but the perverseness of the transgressors shall destroy them" (Proverbs 11:3).

Self-control

If you want to make it in life, lay hold on self-control and make room for it.

"A man that has no rule over his own spirit is like a city that is broken down and without a wall" (Proverbs 25:29).

Self-control is the essence of life. You cannot serve God in spirit and truth if you cannot subject yourself to discipline. Hear what King David said in Psalm 101:2-3:

"I will behave myself wisely in a perfect way, oh when will thou come unto me? I will walk within my house with a perfect heart. I will set no wicked thing before mine eyes. I hate the work of them that turn aside; it shall not cleave to me"

A man without self-control cannot possess the dominion mandate God originally intended for mankind.

Knowledge

Another important room you must create is the room of knowledge:

"Good understanding gives favour" (Proverbs 13:15).

This will help you greatly in your relationship with God. If you have knowledge, every request you make will be with understanding.

A life that is full of the knowledge of truth will not stumble in the dark (ignorance is darkness). If you do not possess the knowledge of God, everything that transpires between you and your children on board your ark will be a mere transfer of ignorance.

Excellence

Always go for quality and do not allow anyone to despise your uniqueness. *Excellence is your key to advancement;* make room for it. Go for the best. Invest time and effort in everything you do. They will pay off in the end.

"Seest thou a man diligent in his business, he shall stand before kings, he shall not stand before mean men" (Proverbs 22:19).

Improvement

Create a room for improvement in your life and be willing to learn at all times. If you do this, there will be no limit to your success potential. *Those who keep on learning will keep on growing, and those who keep on growing will keep on bearing fruit.*

Determination

Be determined to fulfil your purpose in life. Start working on your vision. Write that book. Establish that business. Birth new things into existence. Travail, push and give birth to purpose. Chance favours the trained mind. If you are determined to succeed, the host of hell will not succeed in stopping you. Nothing can stop what God has ordained to come to pass in your life.

Remember, God ordered you to make "rooms". There are many more you can create. Just be sure all the rooms are God-centred and not people-centred. God has asked you to make "rooms" and not "relationships". If you build a relationship with people who cannot create, they stand to *cremate* what you *create*.

No More Room!

Here lies wisdom: Give "no room" for laziness in your life! "No room" for wickedness! "No room" for sin! "No room" for time-wasters!

Many people enter into unnecessary relationships that land them in chaos simply because they do not want to be alone. Understand, however, that success requires the ability to *be* alone. You do not need people to get attracted to you. Get attracted to yourself. Not everybody will celebrate you so celebrate yourself.

You do not have space for aimless pursuits. Make room for God's purpose; pursue it and you will succeed.

<u>WISDOM PRINCIPLES</u>

*All things end well that start and
progress with God.
Therefore, let God be the first and last
in all you do - this is the secret of success.*

*Absolute obedience enhances
divine intervention.*

*If God gives you an assignment,
adhere strictly to the
Master-Designer's specifications;
don't do it any other way.*

*Create room for improvement in your ark and
leave no room for aimlessness.*

3   Fortified
Inside Out

G OD commanded Noah to build an ark. He gave him the blueprints for construction. He specified the type of wood for the ark and told him to "make rooms". Notice the next thing God said: *"Pitch it within and without with a pitch"* (Genesis 6:14c). In other words, God ordered Noah to "fortify" the ark within and without. He also had a *sequence* in mind — inside the ark and *then* outside the ark.

Noah was told to strengthen the inner parts of the ark and afterwards strengthen the outside. This instruction is relevant for today's "ark builder".

Inside vs. Outside

The *inside* of the ark relates directly to those who will reside in the ark (relational attitudes which depend on character development), while the *outside* relates to the frequent contact with the waters and storms of life. It is therefore important to strengthen the *inside* of the ark and make it habitable, bearing in mind that different types of "creatures" will pass through your ark for survival.

It breaks my heart when I see people focusing more on their outward appearance than their inner life; people who work more on their public reputation than their private disposition.

Such people love sanctimonious greetings in the marketplace, just as the Pharisees did. They pose as angels on the outside but stink like graves on the inside. Many homes are full of strife, hatred, destructive criticism and all sorts of abomination, but outwardly, they show off as happy, lovely people.

Inner Fortification

No preacher has the right to command others to obey God when his entire household is rebellious against God. You cannot show others the way to Canaan when your children are heading towards Egypt. Fortify your family life first. Raise a standard of love, peace and respect in your home. Only then would you succeed in strengthening your public life.

Lately, I have discovered that the crowd that attends Church conferences, retreats or seminars is not an accurate assessment of the internal strength of a congregation. What is important to God is the internal life of an assembly and how the believers relate with each other.

The Holy Spirit dwells in your heart, but if you harbour filthiness in your mind, He would not be comfortable in you. No one other than yourself (and the Lord) knows your thoughts and meditations. If your mind is carnal, your "ark" may not survive the constant bombardment of immorality and worldly lusts.

Your public life may form the basis of people's assessment of you, but understand that God judges who we are on the inside. Anyone can put up a good show to impress others. People practice wickedness under a mask of piety. God, however, cannot be mocked; He will judge the wickedness of men at the coming of the Lord.

Are you strong on the inside? How steadfast is your relationship with God? Are you a person of integrity and character? I have good news for you: *It is not too late for you to fortify your inner life.*

Amend your ways *now*. Make the crooked ways straight in your life. God knows you from the inside out. Be transparent before Him.

Outer Fortification

When you are strong on the inside, no devil can contend with you on the outside. You will be able to withstand the storms of satanic attacks and peoples' opinion.

"And God shut him in"

When your life is adequately fortified, God will shut you in as He did Noah. Even when you do not know what the Lord is doing, stay "shut in" and watch God act on your behalf.

"Being confident of this very thing, that he which hath begun a good work in you will perform it until the day of Jesus Christ" (Philippians 1:6).

Whenever God shuts you in, remain "shut in". Do not succumb to the attractiveness of your environment. Do not seek companionship when God wants you for Himself. Only one bad relationship is enough to sink the ark of your destiny.

When you experience the splash of waters on the outside of your ark, do not fear; the fortifications will prove strong enough. With God you can relax and cruise on the storms of life.

WISDOM PRINCIPLES

You do not need a crowd to be successful.
You can be surrounded by a crowd
and yet be alone

Be good inside out.

Know yourself and know the God in you. This is the
secret of self-confidence.

Stay "shut-in" with God, even when you don't
know what He is doing.

Just one unwarranted relationship is enough to sink
the ark of your destiny.

Do not fear the splash of water against your ark.
Relax and cruise the storm —
it's a dynamic mobility towards your destiny.

4 Never Stay Out Of Fashion

T HE wisdom of God is unfathomable. He exists from eternity past. Before the beginning began; before the foundation of the earth was laid, He is God. He declared through His prophet, *"I am the Lord, I changeth not" (Malachi 3:6)*. He is the unchangeable changer and the timeless timer. As He was in the beginning so He is and so shall He be, times without end. He framed the whole world by His word and created man in His own image.

Unlike God, everything in this world lapses. The best car in town twenty years ago is "out of fashion" today. The magnificent building that stood as a landmark forty-seven years ago is now an antique. Technology changes with time. The world, over the years, has witnessed tremendous changes in ecology, politics and socio-economics.

If you approach life the way it used to be,

people will label you "old fashion". Everything around you, except God, is *subject* and *expected* to change. The world *expects* you to go with the flow. However, instead of going with the world's flow, you can go with God's. His flow is never-ending. His word, though settled in heaven, is never out of fashion!

Everything grows old and fades away, but God's word remains the same. It is new every morning. Whatever God commands you to do will never go out of fashion. He knows the end from the beginning. He is the Alpha and Omega. The destiny He packaged for you will remain relevant as long as you follow His leading and keep to His blueprint.

Nobody has the same fingerprint as yours. This is sufficient proof that you cannot get out of fashion as long as you follow the specifications for your ark! If only you are willing and obedient, you will enjoy the best in the land.

Specific Measurements

God gave Noah *specific* measurements for the Ark and expected him to adhere strictly to them. God said, *"This is the **fashion** which thou* *shalt make it of" (Genesis 6:15)*, and went ahead to give the length, breadth and height of the ark.

The "length", "breadth" and "height" of your achievements are dependent on your obedience to God's commands. In this context, your destiny is in your hand because if you obey God, you will have good success, but if you do not, failure is sure. *Make sure you measure up to expectation and do not out-run God's programme for your life.* Do not be over-ambitious and thus miss God's specific measurement.

When you exceed God's "measurements" for your life; when you step beyond the boundaries of God's instructions, He will proceed to prune the excesses out of your life. He will subject you to tribulations of many kinds just to conform you to His perfect will.

For God to build you up experientially, He would subject you to tribulation. You would pass through a fiery furnace. However, one thing is sure, He will be with you in the fire of affliction. This will develop your experience, get you out of mediocrity and move you into perfection. God is not going to release wealth to you when you are not mature enough to maintain it.

"Our fathers disciplined us for a little while as they thought best; but God disciplines us for our good, that we may share in his holiness. No discipline seems pleasant at the time, but painful. Later on, however, it produces a harvest of righteousness and peace for those who have been trained by it" (Hebrews 12:10,11).

Achieving fame is not difficult, but you need character to sustain you there. A godly character will never go out of fashion.

The Three Decks

The fashion of Noah's ark included the construction of three decks - the lower, middle and higher decks. These decks were significant; they all fulfilled a purpose.

Each day, time is ordered in three stages— morning, afternoon and evening. The process of living is also in three phases—infancy, adolescence and old age. Applying this understanding to the pursuit of purpose, it is easy to see that the journey towards destiny starts from an *elementary* stage, to an *intermediate* stage and finally, to an *advanced* stage.

In view of the fact that you will encounter and accommodate different types of "creatures" in your ark, it is important to build your lives on "three levels". The wisdom of this admonition is applicable in different areas of life.

Relationships

Generally, you relate with people over different time periods. Some relationships are short, some are for fairly longer periods, and others are on a permanent basis. You need to discern the nature of every relationship you enter into. Jesus did not entrust himself to man because He discerned man's thoughts and intents (John 2:24,25).

When you are "young" and inexperienced in life, you find it easy to accommodate just anybody. This is your "first deck".

As you grow to manhood, realise the need to drop some ideas, mentalities and even *relationships* to the lower "deck". Abraham had to part with Lot in order to move into the. promises of God for His life. This is the time to prioritise your time. Your family must come first, after God. Do not focus on your business at the expense of family relationships. Spend time with your spouse and children. A strong family unit will survive the strongest of storms.

The highest relationship level you want to maintain is your walk with God. Nothing should interfere with this on the "third deck".

Family

The need to build a strong family cannot be over-emphasised. Noah entered the ark with his entire family. Claim the promise of salvation for every member of your home (Acts 16:31).

Waste no time "downstairs" with people who do not *add* to you. Invest on your children. Do not expose them to the "beasts" on the lower deck. Raise a standard of morality and excellence in your home. Grow with your family into all that God has ordained for you.

Be one with your partner on the "third deck". Turn your bedroom into a sanctuary of love. True love will survive the fires of affliction. The Bible affirms that *"Many waters cannot quench love, neither can the floods drown it"* (Song of Solomon 8:7).

Do not argue in front of your children on the "second deck". Be an example of peace and harmony. Allow no "third party" (especially the in-laws!) to interfere with your affairs. Restrict them to the "third deck".

In short, make your family life a top priority. This is a major key that sustains success.

Prayer

Develop a strong habit of prayer. The first prayer deck you want to build is *corporate prayer* — your times of prayer with other people in Church, meetings and conferences. The second prayer deck is *family prayer* — your times of prayer with your partner and children. The third prayer deck is *personal prayer* — your personal time with God.

Spend more time alone with God. Stay connected with Him. Your relationship with others depends on your relationship with God. The things you learn from God and His Word, impress *first* on your children and family.

Admonish your children not to imitate the world. Train them to resist the influence of the "beasts" in your ark. The One they should imitate is God, their Maker.

Never Out of Fashion

You have been fashioned for excellence by your Fashion-Designer, the Almighty God. His way of doing things is best. Keep to His instructions and create no new design for yourself. His calculations are the best. When you build according to His revealed pattern, you will never go out of fashion.

"Thus did Noah; according to ALL that God commanded him, so did he".

<u>WISDOM PRINCIPLES</u>

God 'fashioned' you for success;
Do not stay out of fashion.

You are a sum total of what He fashioned
you to be. Keep to His divine measurements,
structure and shape.

Life is ordered in three stages – infancy, adolescence
and manhood.. Recognise the different phases of life
you will have to pass through and act appropriately.

Don't live aimlessly.
Set a standard for your personal life and home.

Recognise that some people are in transit
in your life - they will soon leave.

Make sure you complete your assignment
before God calls you home.

5

The Stink
or the Storm

OUR God is faithful. He knows all things and can do all things. To Him belongs all knowledge. He provided Noah with the know-how of building the ark. For success, Noah depended solely on God.

You do not need archives of experience to start building your life. Your primary need is absolute obedience to the commands of God. If you rely on the wisdom of God, you will achieve success. Apostle Paul declared, *"I can do all things through Christ which strengtheneth me" (Philippians 4:13).*

You can do all things as well if you rely on Christ's strength. Stand firm on your feet and negate every "I-cannot-do-it" thought. Resist the devil and he will flee from you. Do not allow little things to frustrate you. Stand your ground and obey God. It may be difficult, but do not give up. Quitters do not win; winners do not quit. Reach out in faith and step with confidence into the realm of possibilities, for with God all things are possible (Luke 1:37).

Don't Stop Your Achievements

When you complete the construction of your ark, everybody would see how marvellous it is. Some will criticise your achievements. Others will wonder how it all happened. *You should know, however, that there is much more to be done.*

The ark that Noah built had nothing to propel it neither was it fitted with a steam engine. It needed the power of God for mobility. Are you at this stage of part-achievement? Do not make the mistake of stopping at you present accomplishment; go to the next level. *Your present achievement is not a guarantee for future exploits. Be willing, therefore, to face further challenges.*

After Noah finished building the ark he had nothing else to do than obey God's instruction to bring in the animals two by two. Likewise, while you wait for God's direction, keep on doing what He already commanded you to do.

Stand by your ark and welcome in the beasts. Load food for yourself, your family and for the animals. Load in not a few for the journey may be long. Do not give up; keep loading. When you load enough food to last your flooding period, get inside your ark, and wait for God to shut the door!

Do not bother about moving your ark. *The flood is the fuel for your ark and the storm is the propeller!* Perhaps its seems as though nothing is moving in your life; everything is at a standstill; you have been at your work-place for years without any promotion; frustration is setting in and hope is growing dim. Do not panic! Your grounded ark will soon experience a lift by a great storm!

When the storm starts, it will seem like a great shake-up. Even the ark would sway as though it's going to break into pieces. Fear not, God is with you. He knows what is happening and what *He* is doing.

Ride the Storms

Noah was not a professional sailor. He had no compass to determine his geographical movements. There was no steering control fitted on the ark. He had no idea of where he was going, where he wanted to go or how fast he was travelling.

Perhaps you sense some "movement" in your life but you have no control over what is happening. Remain calm and cast all your burdens on the One who can sustain you. You are not *sailing;* rather, you are *staying* afloat the storms of life. This is the purpose of the ark.

Be conscious of those who have taken refuge in your "ark". There survival depends on the survival of your ark. Depend totally on God and pay the price of sparing lives.

Patience

The bridge between God's promise and its fulfilment is *Patience.* Noah lived in the ark for one whole year. Have you waited that long? Be assured in your mind—you will ride the storm and not sink! God will not forget you no matter how long your stormy period lasts.

Unusual Deliverance

After five months of turbulence, Noah adapted to life in the ark and *on* the storm.

When God saw that Noah was used to riding without fear, God ushered him to the next level.

"And God remembered Noah, and every living thing, and all the cattle that was with him in the ark, and God made a wind to pass over the ark and the waters asswaged" (Genesis 8:1).

Imagine the type of wind that can dry up the waters that covered the whole earth. For Noah, this was another terrible experience. His *usual* experience on the water was replaced with the *unusual*. God is the *Unusual God*. In whatever situation you find yourself, trust God because He is in charge. ***If God gives you a ridiculous instruction, He is actually setting you up for a miraculous intervention!***

Always prepare your heart to give *strange* obedience to *strange* instructions in order to facilitate *strange* positive results. When the unusual happens, especially after much prayer and absolute dependence on God, do not panic; that's part of the deliverance package. All you need to do is contact the control tower. The unusual God will use the unusual means to remove the unusual sound that terrorises you and land your ark safely in an unusual manner.

Life in the Ark

Imagine living in a zoo with a variety of animals! In Noah's Ark, there were only eight people and thousands of beasts. They all lived together for 365 days. How horrible it must have been for Noah and his family to live with birds, snakes, lions, to mention but a few.

Noah certainly had no time for socialising. They had to cope with the sounds and demands of the animals. Noah did not only feed the animals, but also had to bear with their various mannerisms. Some acted so dumb and others too smart.

You will also have different kinds of people to deal with in your life. Different kinds of people with diverse characters will pass through your life. The following animals in Noah's ark probably describe some of them.

"Gorillas"

There are people like gorillas who never seem to be serious in their life. They love unprofitable conversations and do not respect your time. If you are a person of purpose, you will find it difficult to associate with such people. Paul admonished Timothy many times to shun foolish talk. It's a good advice for you to keep also.

"Elephants"

Some people are "big" as elephants, but exhibit no maturity. They are shallow-minded and highly irritating in their attitude. Do not expect too much from them lest you get disappointed. Do not judge people by their outward appearance. Many put up an act to impress. Discern the real person behind every mask by the help of God's Spirit.

"Tigers and lions"

Tigers and Lions will also pass through your "ark". They live to satisfy their appetites. If you allow such people to depend on you for their livelihood, they will never learn dependence on God. Cease being the "Alpha and Omega" of people's needs. On the long run, it is more profitable to teach someone how to fish than to give him a three-course fish meal.

"Grasshoppers"

What about people with grasshopper mentalities? When you are singing "standing on the promises of God", they are "standing on the doubts of their minds"! Grasshoppers see themselves inferior to others and far from success. (Numbers 13:1-29). They do not eat grapes, but prefer the food of Egypt.

Grasshoppers do not see themselves in the centre of God's will. They see themselves, instead, in the centre of defeat. They consider themselves a failure before any attempt towards success. These kind of people are full of evil reports, have no faith in God, always rebel and wage war against the willing soul.

The Grasshopper spirit is contagious. It dwells on the past, despises the present and destroys the future. People with grasshopper mentalities do not wish themselves any good, neither do they plan for their descendants. For them, success is an abomination. Their common language is "I cannot do it", "we cannot make it", thus reducing themselves to nothing before others. They never survive wilderness experiences.

Grasshoppers perpetrate evil in words and in deeds, they instigate it, influence and master-mind it. Because they are not willing and obedient, they cannot eat the good of the land.

This class of people occupy space in your ark and you need wisdom to deal with them.

"Swine"

Another class of beasts that I would like to examine is the "swine". All pigs know to do is murmur all day and eat without stop. They eat just anything, including junk food.

They always want to enjoy the benefit of your own effort but never want to pay any price. Anything is food to the pigs, they have no self-control. Swine don't take a bath so you have to get used to the way they stink.

"Swine" hate neatness and love filthiness. Do not wrestle with them or you will get dirty. Swine have a bad character. They have no defence against possible attack and when they are attacked once, they run violently into destruction. Waste no time thinking about their abnormal behaviours in the ark, that's their way of life.

"Giraffes"

The giraffe class of people are inquisitive, nosy and busy-bodies. Because of their "long necks", they assume they have the right to know everything that goes on in your life. Without an invitation, they use their privileged position to spy into your privacy and liberty. They may despise you and make you feel that you need them to navigate your way through life. Do not be intimidated because God will help you achieve what you were created to accomplish for His glory.

Endure the stink

Can you imagine the atmosphere inside the ark? There were no bathrooms, no toilets, and the animals kept breeding, producing more "trouble" after their kinds! Everywhere was filled with repulsive odours and yet Noah could not do away with the animals!

Moreover, virtually all the animals had peculiar and irritating characters that made Noah feel like giving up in the middle of the flood. However, if he had quit, he would have had a decision to make: to endure the *stink* in the ark, or *sink* in the flood. What is God teaching us here? That the secret of survival and eventual success is *endurance*. To succeed in life, we must learn how to endure all things. If we endure now, we will enjoy later.

In this respect, our Lord Jesus is a role model for us to emulate:

"Let this mind be in you, which was also in Christ Jesus: who, being in the form of God thought it not robbery to be equal with God, but made himself of no reputation, and took upon him the form of a servant, and was made in the likeness of men. And being found in 'fashion' as a man, he humbled himself and became obedient unto death, even the death of the cross. Therefore God also hath highly exalted Him, and given him a name which is above every name: That at the name of Jesus every knee should bow, of things in heaven, and things in earth, and things under the earth, and that every tongue should confess that Jesus Christ is Lord to the Glory of God the Father" (Philippians 2:5-11).

You can either endure the stink in your ark or perish in the storm. The stink you are experiencing from undesirable occupants of your ark cannot kill you. God is teaching you a lesson of endurance. He wants you to get familiar with peoples' unprecedented way of life, and the best time to know people is when they are packed together with you in your ark. It is either the stink or the storm, so learn how to endure hardship as a good soldier of Christ.

Endure the stink in the ark because in a short while, your ark will land and the beasts will be out of your life and you will enjoy the freshness of a new life. ***Endurance is the key to success.***

<u>WISDOM PRINCIPLES</u>

You do not need to be experienced before you start building your life. Experience comes as you obey God's instructions.

Don't drop out at the face of frustration. Refuse to quit.

Have a short celebration of your achievements and move on.

If your ark is ready and you don't know what to do next, keep loading.

If you are anxious about how your ark will move, you are trying to outrun God. just wait, the storm is coming. The flood is fuel for your ark, and the storm is its propeller.

The bridge between God's promise and

its fulfilment is 'patience'

You have only two options:
the stink in the ark or the storm outside.
Choose the stink; it will not last forever

Prepare your mind;
the storm that lifts your ark up is a lot easier than
the force that keeps you going.

6 Help! My Patience Is Running Out!

I N whatever position we find ourselves, God is dealing with us as sons. When he subjects us to difficult circumstances, he knows that the end is glorious. He is never in a hurry.

It is said that "there is a limit to human endurance". Do you know the reason why? Because it is "human endurance" and not "God's". Human endurance is not divine because it is void of hope and where there is no hope, faith is dormant.

"Faith is the substance of things hoped for, the evidence of things not seen" (Hebrews 11:1).

Tired of the Ark?

Are you tired of life in the ark? Are you finding it difficult. to bear with the different "animals"? Are you weary of the turbulence created by the storm? Be encouraged; it is not yet time for you to run out of patience. It's too late to fail. *If your patience is truly running out, go to God and cry out for help!*

God will strengthen you. He is the very present help in the day of trouble. Perhaps you need a little rest before you push again. Just look up, here stands the Master-Designer beside your bed of travail, hold on to him—He designed you for success.

Consider Jesus Christ, the Saviour of mankind. He knew who He was and why He came to the world. Yet, He held His peace for thirty years before His ministry began. Were there no sick bodies around Him during His waiting time? Didn't people die that He could bring back to life? Wasn't the Solution to people's problems mistaken to be the carpenter's son?

What Jesus demonstrated to us was the need for patience as we wait on God's timing. You can anchor your hope in Christ even in times of Crisis? *Patience is the bridge on which you will walk from God's promises to their fulfilment.*

"But they that wait upon the Lord shall renew their strength; they shall mount up with wings as eagles,. they shall run and not be weary, and they shall walk and not faint" (Isaiah 40:31).

The Ark Rested

"And the Ark 'rested' on the seventh month, on the seventeenth day of the month, upon the mountains of Ararat" (Genesis 8:4).

Note carefully that the ark *rested;* it did not *land.* There is a great disparity between the two. As you wait upon the Lord and renew your strength, God will grant you a "temporary landing" so that both the ark and the entire occupants can *rest* and prepare for the last lap of the journey.

Perhaps your ark is now resting on the mountains of "Ararat"; this is not the time to celebrate safe arrival. You will still have to land safely on dry ground. Remember, Noah's "storm and wind experience" lasted a whole year and afterwards, the ark *rested* on mount Ararat on the seventh month. He still spent another five months in the ark before a more powerful wind prepared him for landing.

Do not attempt to outrun God. His programme for your life is divine. Resist the temptation of getting off mount "Ararat". It is not, yet time for you to come out of the ark. The door must not be opened. The covering of the ark must remain intact. Do not sound the victory alarm yet.

Take Stock

Rather, this is a season of refill, a time for you to fasten your loose belts and get more secured in your purpose. This is a time to take stock and carry out spiritual checks and balances; a time to encourage yourself and crew members in the Lord. It's also a time to cross-examine the beast-occupants of the ark. This is the time you will discover that scorpions have produced, monkeys are pregnant and pigs in the process of birthing a new stink!

Focus on God through Prayer

You will discover that the horrible sound of waters splashing on your ark will cease immediately your ark rests on the mountain. This is an opportunity to focus squarely on God through prayer. The period on your Ararat is a time you move to your penthouse on the "third floor" with your family to renew your strength in God. Get away from interferences of the "ground-floor".

Tap into the reservoir of power. Give more attention to prayer at this time and unto the study of the word of God. He will speak into your life.

Resist the devil

As you wait on God, it may seem as though nothing is happening on the mountain. You will not feel any motion. Capitalising on the moment, satan will whisper intimidating words into your heart. He will tempt you to jump out of the ark before the appointed time. This is the time to declare war against him! Stand tall in the Lord and decree the word of God against him. Resist the devil and he will flee away from you (James 4:8).

Do Not Give Up!

The worst thing that can happen to anyone aspiring for success is to give up just before crossing the finish line. Whenever you are despairing of strength to move on, get on your knees and shout to God for help. Do not be ashamed to cry, "Lord, my patience is running out!" God has promised a renewal of strength to those who call on Him.

I have reached the "giving up point" many times, but each time I go to God and cry for help, God fills my heart with joy and hope that cannot be described. He strengthens my bones and His dynamic power comes mightily upon me. With this, I have the courage to go extra miles.

When Elijah cried to the Lord for help, (I Kings 19:4), God strengthened him. Moses ran away from Egypt and had his own Ararat experience under Jethro of Median. When the Lord restored his strength, he went back to Egypt and faced circumstances worse than the one he ran away from.

The Israelites, on the other hand, could not endure their "Ararat season". They murmured and rebelled against God — and perished in the wilderness.

Maintain Your Confession

While you are resting on mountain Ararat, keep on making positive confessions. Declare it with confidence: *I am designed for success! I am not a failure. Its too late to give up. I have paid a price, and whatever more it will cost me, I stand without compromise.*

Strengthen yourself in the word of God. Fight a good fight with the prophecies you have received. The adversaries of the Lord shall be broken into pieces before you. Let the Redeemed of the Lord say so! If God be with you, who can be against you? The joy of the Lord is your strength. Cast all your burdens on God, and He will sustain you. Remember, you are not alone in the ark, the Master Designer is with you. You will soon get off your "Ararat" and in a short while, land safely at your Port of Destiny — which is your expected end.

Remain "Shut In"

When Noah and the animals first entered the ark, the Bible noted that God "shut him in". Now, after the ark rested on the mountains of Ararat, Noah did not open the window of the ark until after forty days of staying on a spot.

"And it came to pass at the end of forty days, that Noah opened the window of the ark which he had made" (Genesis 8:6).

If you do not know what to do at a particular point in life, stay "shut in" with the Lord. Trying to force yourself into action brings chaos. When God gives you an instruction, stick to it no matter how long and make sure you do not manipulate circumstances to quicken the time.

Don't Rely on People

After Noah opened the window of the ark, he sent out two birds to survey the land (Genesis 8:6-9). He first sent out a *raven* and then a *dove.*

These two birds are completely different from each other. The raven is a selfish and greedy bird while the dove is gentle and harmless. When Noah sent out the raven, it flew to and fro until the waters abated. The dove, on the other hand, came back to the ark twice but never returned the third time. This goes to prove that only God is ultimately reliable. To trust in men—even "good" men— is not wise.

When things are difficult in your life, do not rely on what man can do for you. People you have helped in the past will "fly away" from you and never return. Do not be offended. You have eagle-wings, so quit relying on the wings of "ravens" or "doves".

If the "ravens" and "doves" in your life decide to fly away, let them go. They are not supposed to do your "flying" for you in the first place.

Do not see through another person's eyes. Begin to see life through your own God-given eyes. To see far and wide, see through the eyes of God.

If you can see what the future holds for you, even with the absence of some people, then you can have it. Abraham could not see the land until Lot departed from his life.

*"And the LORD said unto Abram, **after that Lot was separated from him**, Lift up now thine eyes, and look from the place where thou art northward, and southward, and eastward, and westward: **For all the land which thou seest, to thee will I give it, and to thy seed for ever"** (Genesis 13:14,15).*

Get ready to possess your land. Be patient in the face of disappointment because God is working things out to favour you.

<u>WISDOM PRINCIPLES</u>

*Patience is the bridge on which you will
walk from God's promises to their fulfilment.*

*Train your mind to stand still —
the Omnipotent God is never in a hurry.*

*Don't run out of patience;
anxiety can capsize your ship of destiny.*

*Your "Ararat" is a place of waiting
until God moves again. Your resting period on the
mountain is not the time to celebrate save arrival.*

*Celebrate the exit of some people from your life and
move on to your next phase.*

If you can see it you can have it.

7 The Landing Storm

T HERE are three "storm" stages in life that affect anyone with a purpose and destiny. The *first* is called the "flood wave". This is the strong force that lifts your ark off the ground and initiates the purpose for which the ark was made.

The *second* storm is the "cruising force". This is a terrible wind that keeps the ark going on the sea of life. It is a dynamic propelling force that moves you forward on a high speed at the face of trouble. While your faith fuels the ark, the "cruising force" keeps you going. At this stage, no one can regulate the speed of your ark except the Almighty God.

The *third* storm stage is the most difficult. This is called "The landing storm". The storm that lifts your ark and the one that keeps it afloat during the flood period, is far easier than the storm that lands the ark at the port of destiny. *The most difficult storm in life is the landing storm.*

Noah's Deliverance

In Genesis chapter 8:1 the Bible says:

"And God remembered Noah, and every living thing, and all the cattle that was with him in the ark; and God made a wind to pass over the earth, and the waters asswaged".

God remembered Noah after five months of floating on water. He was ready to fulfil His promise to Noah—the promise to sustain him and his family. Noah's deliverance was about to come but he did not have a clue *how* it was coming. God sent a great wind to blow over the whole earth - a wind powerful enough to dry off the waters from the surface of the earth. It was even greater than a whirlwind. I call it the "landing wind".

Having spent five months on the flood, Noah got used to life in the ark. The stink became the norm to him. He had mastered how to handle the animals. The waves and the wind did not affect him anymore. He had become a master of his circumstances. God had to upset his comfort zone by sending the "landing storm".

Birth Pains

Just as the pain of contraction cannot compare with the travail of childbirth, the "cruising force" is milder than the "landing storm". Be prepared to travail before your God-given ideas materialise. *You will feel the greatest pain just before your destiny breaks forth.*

There are stages in life when it appears as if God no longer answers prayer. All you receive after months of prayer and fasting is a single promise from God, "It shall happen *soon!*" In response, you ask the question: "How *soon* is soon?". If you are presently in this type of a dilemma, remain calm; God cares for you. There is no other way to your landslide victory but through the "landing storm".

Remember, you want to possess the *land* and not the *waters* that cover the land. The waters must, therefore, recede from the earth, and the wind that will make this possible must be fierce. One thing you can be sure of: you *will* land safely. When your problems get more complicated as you pray, your ark is about to land.

I have seen God intervene in the circumstances of many people. In almost every case, things will *first* seem to get out of hand, *especially* when the breakthrough is just about to come. At the very last minute, when the pressure is most unbearable, the tide turns.

God is never late nor early. He is *always on* time. Your situation may stretch you to a final breaking point, but be sure, you will not *break.* It may seem hopeless, but do not give up hope. A great calm will follow the raging of the landing storm.

God is With You

The solution to our problems often come en-route a fiery furnace. If after waiting patiently for God, things get harder and more confusing, do not cease to believe that God is *able* to move on your behalf. God *will* take care of the situation, but you cannot dictate the "how" and "when" to Him.

No matter how tough the wind is, always remember that the Master-Designer is there with you. He did not ordain for you to perish in the storms of life. He has established His covenant with you. You are designed for success. When the "landing storm" comes, all you need is absolute dependence on God. Stay connected to your Main Source. Fasten your seat belt and get ready for the final landing.

If God will not complete His purpose in your life, He will not start it. He has declared the end from the beginning (Isaiah 46:10). In a short while, you will hear the victorious announcement: *Welcome to your success destination!*

<u>WISDOM PRINCIPLES</u>

The storm that lands you into success is more fierce than the storm that starts you up.

The greater the problem, the bigger the victory.

You are to possess the land, not the flood, and God will use whatever it takes to clear the waters and give you the land.

It's always rocky on the boat of life; remember, you are anchored in Christ.

Stay connected to your control tower; fasten your seatbelt because you are close to the port!

8

Exiting The Ark

NOAH'S ark landed safely. The waters dried off the earth completely. A phase in Noah's *life ended* and another was to *start*. The ark fulfilled its purpose and Noah was ready to abandon it for his next assignment.

When a phase of your life ends, move into the next. The wife of the prophet operated this principle; whenever a vessel was filled with oil, she set it aside for another empty one. You cannot build a monument around your present achievements. You must proceed to the next phase of your life.

The ark is meant to carry you across the flood and land you safely on dry ground. It is not a permanent abode for your family to live in. Outside the ark, there is an endless expanse of land for you to possess. Will you remain in the ark?

Do Not Rush

"And Noah removed the covering of the ark, and looked, and behold, the face of the ground was dry" (Genesis 8:13b).

Noah did not rush out of the ark. He removed, first of all, the covering of the ark, and surveyed the earth. I cherish Noah's wisdom here. He did not step out of the ark until God gave him new instructions. Friend, I know you have a divine appointment, but if you want God's ultimate intervention, always wait for divine direction.

Instead of rush out of the ark, Noah removed "the covering" of the ark. What does this mean to you? Life in the ark is quite different from life on the ground. When the "covering" of the ark is removed, fresh air comes into the ark. After landing, remove the covering of your ark to allow fresh ideas into your mind. Discover the greater potentials that you have. View the endless opportunities that lie before you.

After spending a year in a closed ark, you need fresh inspiration for fresh dominion. You are no longer restricted to the pattern of life in the ark. You can now possess the land, have dominion and subdue the earth.

"Go forth from the ark, thou and thy wife, and thy sons, and thy sons wives with thee" (Genesis 8:15).

Noah and his family came out of the ark first, and then all the beasts came out and headed straight into the bush. No one looked back to appreciate Noah and his family for taking care of them; there was no "thank you".

As you stepped into the wisdom of God to build the ark (which no one else had ever built), so you must step into God's wisdom to start a new life *outside the ark.* Make sure all the "beasts" depart from your life as well! They no longer form part of your company but rather they are meat for your consumption!

Be Wise

The fact that you once accommodated all kinds of "animals" in your ark does not mean you should form alliances with them. When it is time to exit the ark, let them go to where they belong. It does not matter if they do not thank you for sparing their lives. Be wise in choosing your associates. *You must preserve yourself from being killed by the beasts you saved from death.* Celebrate their departure from your life. Do not feel bad at all. Stay clear of evil association. Guard your life and heart from external contamination.

The flood experience prepared you for greater challenges. You should now be well equipped to deal with all sorts of people. Choose your friends and associates wisely in accordance with God's leading.

Crush the Serpents

Once you step upon dry ground, your land of destiny, beware of the cunningness of serpents and do not associate with them. Rather, obey your God-given mandate to crush their heads:

"And I will put enmity between thee and the woman, between her seed and thy seed; he shall bruise thy head and thou shall bruise his heel" (Genesis 3:15).

There is an ongoing battle between the "offspring" of God and those of the "serpent". You cannot afford to let down your guard nor relax your onslaught. Crush the agendas of evil people and render their activities fruitless.

The way to do this is through prayer, the sword of the Spirit and a close walk with God. Live under the shadow of God's wings and make Him your confidant. When evil men know nothing of your plans anymore, their ability to plot evil with their *minds* is rendered impotent.

Your mandate from God is to crush the heads of serpents. They have the authority to bite you also. Therefore, swing into action quickly before you get bitten.

If given the chance, evil people can stagnate your business, contaminate your ministry or render you spiritually immobile. Be on the alert and frustrate their plans.

The fact that wicked beasts once lived in your ark does not justify their continued association with you. Do not open your heart to everybody. Be quick to hear and slow to answer. This is valuable wisdom for success.

King David prayed in Psalm 140:

"Deliver me Oh Lord from the evil man, preserve me from the violent man; which imagine mischief in their heart; continually are they gathered together for war. They have sharpened their tongues like a serpent; adders'

Designed for Success

poison is under their lips. Keep me Oh Lord from the hands of the wicked, preserve me from the violent man, who have purposed to overthrow my goings. Let not an evil speaker be established in the earth; evil shall hunt the violent man to overthrow him" (Psalm 140:1-4,11).

Be careful of the person who speaks into your life. Learn from the mistakes of others and be wise. If one kind of problem keeps repeating itself in your life, it means you did not learn a lesson in the first occurrence. Get understanding. Life holds all you need, but is not willing to bring it to you. You must reach out and possess your possession.

Live in Your Today

Today is all you have. Only God knows tomorrow. The *yesterday* you spent in the ark was *today* when you were in it; today was *tomorrow* yesterday. Nobody has ever lived in yesterday, neither will anybody live in tomorrow for ever. You have taken an exit from the ark (from your *yesterday*); determine what the new life demands and make the necessary changes.

This is a season of change. You are no longer in the ark propelled by the storm. Take proper control of the affairs of your new life. Remember, immediately the Israelites ate from the fruit of freedom, the manna ceased (Joshua 5:12).

There is no more "manna" for you. It is time to sow seeds and reap a harvest. Rely absolutely on the Holy Spirit's directions. Some instructions will be strange to you, but remember: *strange* obedience to *strange* instructions will yield *strange* and unusual miracles.

Arise and Shine!

Lift up your eyes. What do you see? What can you do with the land before you? Take time to envision the land.

Spread your wings and get ready to soar like an eagle. You are designed for success. Dig deep into the well of knowledge and extract the treasures under the ground. It's all yours.

Think of the new things that you can do. This is a new beginning. It's a new day. Create something new. Take the lead and let others follow. The person who cannot take a step unless he sees another man's footprint will never make a discovery. (Where would Noah have seen another man's footprint after the flood?) What you are designed to do is unique to you; no one else can do or has done it. The first footprint on the surface of the earth after the flood was Noah's. *You* are the best you!

Move forward, there is room for you; why would you be a cheap copy when you are a great original? God has established His covenant with you. Arise and shine for God!

WISDOM PRINCIPLES

When *your ark lands,*
Don't be in a rush to come out.

Adapt to change. Life in the ark is
different from life on the ground.

Once the "beasts" are out of the ark,
celebrate their exit and protect yourself from
possible attacks.

Spare no serpent; crush their heads before they bite
your heel. Block them from penetrating your life
and do not announce the "blocking strategy".
Be faster and wiser than the enemies; be vigilant
because the generation of serpents
have a licence to kill.

Create something. Your God is a Creator
and you also must create. When you are busy
creating, *avoid those who are busy* ***cremating***.

9   *Secrets Of Success*

I love quality and believe the statement, *what is worth doing at all is worth doing well.* If you want to settle for anything at all, always go for gold. Settle for nothing less than the best. Develop a broad mind to take giant steps in doing great things.

As a successful "ark builder", a covenant-keeping child of God and Kingdom-seeking Christian, realise that you still have a long way to go. Celebrate success but not for too long. The success of today is not a guarantee for tomorrow. ***It's good to be an achiever, but never you relent in your efforts to progress.*** All you have achieved so far is a collection of "toys" compared to what God has in stock for you.

"But as it is written, eye have not seen, not ear heard, neither have entered into the heart of

man, the things which God hath prepared for them that love him" (1 Corinthians 2:9).

Always raise the standard in your undertakings. You are not yet a champion if you are a one-time battle winner. Champions are *winning-winners,* people who are used to winning and are known as winners. They are always battle-ready; they never give up until they succeed in the things they lay their hands upon.

Your future is God's history, he knows where you started from and where you are going to end. Remember, He is the Master-Designer of your life. Never run it without Him. God is the only one that knows the extent of your greatness. He knows all about the hidden riches in your life.

You can stand tall on your feet and take back what the devil has stolen away from you. Do you know that the devil is a coward? All he has is tricks; he has no power over you. When you resist him he will flee away from you.

If you want to succeed in life, ***do not settle for just any kind of success.*** Not all good ideas are God's ideas. Not all the wealthy people around the globe are truly successful. Many are successful failures. A success that cannot outlive you is no success. *An achievement that cannot generate breakthroughs for another person is not a success. A success without a successor is a successful failure.*

God is not coming to create wealth for you. You are to create it because He has empowered your hands to do so. He is not a respecter of persons but of principles.

Do not expect a miracle for the things that are within your reach. Take a step of faith and act according to the "fashion" released when God gave you the "Blueprint".

Life in the ark is meant to be a one-off experience. Nobody lives in the ark and goes through such a storm twice. It's a once-in-a-lifetime experience that enables you to acquire a wealth of experience that will see you through other challenges of life.

If you survived the flood and the great storm, what can erosion caused by a little rainfall do to you? Even if you find yourself suddenly in the midst of the Atlantic Ocean tomorrow, stay composed because what you have passed through is by far greater than what the devil wants to put you through. Remember: *You have survived the flood; you will always survive life's challenges.*

Do you know the secret of Joshua's success?
It is the all-time secret of success. Apply it
today — it has never failed:

> *"This book of the Law shall not depart out of
> thy mouth, but thou shall meditate there in day
> and night, that thou may observe to do
> according to all that is written therein: for then
> thou shall make thy way prosperous, and then
> thou shall have good success" (Joshua 1:8).*

Do you want good success? You have a price
to pay. The price of diligent service to God and
steady study of His word. You must desire
strongly the word of God, and be fully
committed to doing what it says.

If you meditate day and night in God's word,
you will know His mind and His statutes will
be engraved in your heart. Not only will you
know it, you will also teach your family and
they will know it too. When God's wish
becomes your command, you will make your
way prosperous.

Search for knowledge. Study to show yourself approved unto God and you will not be put
to shame by ignorance (2 Timothy 2:15).

Always be willing to accept correction. Make room for improvement and do not be reluctant to ask about what you do not know.

Be a great thinker! Great thinkers are great achievers, great achievers are great readers and great readers are great leaders.

Be diligent in the service of the Lord and in your business. King Solomon says in Proverb chapter 22:29: *"Seeth thou a man diligent in his business, he shall stand before kings; he shall not stand before mean men"*.

Give attention to reading. Increase your knowledge base and you will be a person of wisdom.

Whatever you lay your hand upon will prosper if the Lord is pleased with you. Everything Joseph did prospered because the Lord was with him in a strange land. Anywhere you are now is your land of blessing. Remember, wherever the soles of your feet shall tread upon is given unto you. God has designed and packaged you for success.

Protect your "package" under the power of His word. Your "package" is your uniqueness. Never you allow strangers to remove your "package". If you do, there's nothing to attract anyone to what you have in the container. You have something to give the world; something the world desperately needs.

Identify your purpose; write the vision; make it plain on paper and others will run with it (Habakkuk 2:2). *"For the vision is yet for an appointed time, but at the end it shall speak and not lie: though it tarry, wait for it; because it will surely come, it will not tarry" (verse 3).*

You can do that business; you can write that book; there are great music albums in you; take a step *now*. If you fail to fulfil destiny, you have not only robbed yourself, but have wounded many others whose source of livelihood are tied to your breakthrough.

It's time for you to release the reservoir in you, burst out and let the river of success water the dry ground around you. You have many people to influence to the Lord. Noah obeyed God and he saved lives. You have lives to save as well. Start now and influence nations for Jesus Christ.

Apostle Paul said in Philippians 3:13: *Brethren, I count not myself to have apprehended, but this one thing I do, forgetting those things which are behind, and reaching forth unto those things which are before. I press toward the mark for the prize of the high calling of God in Christ Jesus.*

Work hard and press toward the future. Press toward excellence, and your integrity will create a reputation for soundness.

Let go of the past. Do not tie yourself to the stigma of past failures. Do not build the foundation of your future on past experiences. Even if you failed, you are not a failure.

Every successful person in the world today had one time or the other tried and failed. *Failure is an evidence of your willingness to succeed.* The greatest mistake on earth is to be afraid to make one.

You are designed for success! Take up your blueprints and start construction. Let all hell come against you, you are more than a conqueror. Nothing can separate you from the love of Christ (Romans 8:35).

Determine to be a finisher. Jesus Christ, your role model, is a Finisher. You can be a finisher too. Nehemiah *finished* the building of the walls of Jerusalem; you will finish the construction work in your life. Paul finished his ministerial assignment; you will accomplish the task ahead.

Confess everyday: *I am a finisher, I will not die half-way. Apostle Paul finished his course, I will finish mine.*

Chance favours the *trained mind.* If you train your mind for absolute breakthrough, you will have it.

Destroy the devil's greatest weapon called fear. Fear not, for I am with thee saith the Lord. For God has not given us the spirit of fear but of power, love, and a sound mind (2 Timothy 1:7).

What God has designed you to be, no devil can stop; powers and principalities cannot stop it. The only person that can stop you from being a success is *yourself.*

If you will stay connected to the Master-Designer, everything is going to be alright.

Take a giant step of faith today, the Master-Designer is with you, even to the end of the world. This is the secret of success.

You are designed for success. It is your life-time mandate!

WISDOM PRINCIPLES

Success without a successor is a successful failure.

Your future is God's history.

Make haste while the sun shines.

*Be a positive thinker. A great thinker is a great
achiever; a great achiever is a great reader and a
great reader is a great leader.*

Be a good example for others to follow.

*You are designed and packaged for success, and
there is nothing better for you to become than
Yourself — this is the secret of success.*

A Prayer for Today's "Ark-Builder"

Father in the mighty Name of Jesus; my glorious Lord I thank you for your love for me. I know that I am designed for success. Your word is leading me to the path of greatness.

Grant me divine revelation in Your word, give me the grace to act according to Your instructions. I decree favour and divine increase upon my life, my home and my business. I step with confidence into the realm of possibilities, and I will go from strength to strength, from power to power, and from glory to glory in Jesus' Name.

Spirit of the Lord, fall afresh on me! I come out with boldness today, and I possess my possession in Jesus' Name. I declare by faith that all is well with me. I am designed for a success and that is settled in heaven! Surely, goodness and mercy shall follow me all the days of my life and I will dwell in the house of the Lord for ever and ever, Amen in Jesus' Name.

10 Final Word: A Call Into The Chamber

HAVING read this book prayerfully, you can now see yourself, I believe, in the centre of God's plan for your life. He has great plans for you—to bless you and make you a blessing. Let nothing stand in the way of your progress. You are *designed for success.*

If you have not surrendered your life to Jesus Christ, *now* is the time to do so. Jesus is the way, the truth and the life. You cannot have peace with the Father except through Him. Accept Jesus as your Lord today and your entire life will change for the better. This is the beginning of a life full of meaning; the true path of greatness.

God is calling you into His chamber. He desires fellowship with you. He will share with you what *true* success is. God does not know failure. As His child, you are *designed for success* and nothing less. Welcome to *His* world of success!

God called me to share *visions of success with people of destiny* and I trust that you are a person of purpose and destiny. If you have decided, through the reading of this book, to entrust your life to God, may I joyfully welcome you into God's success chamber. Congratulations, you are *designed for success.*

HAVE YOU BEEN BLESSED?

To share how this book has blessed you,
or for further information about the author.
and/or prayer assistance,
please contact the author
through the following address:

CLIWOM SANCTUARY OF PRAISE
709 Old Kent Road
London SE15 1JJ
Tel: 020 7358 9994
Fax: 020 7358 9992
Email: ajitena@hotmail.com

*CLIWOM SANCTUARY OF PRAISE is a full
liberation ministry and a church where we share
visions of success with people of destiny.*

The *Emmanuel House* Vision:

Spreading the knowledge
of God's glory to the ends of the earth
by raising writers
and releasing classics;

Expounding the mind of God
for this present generation;

Motivating and inspiring
God's people towards
reality, purpose and destiny.